Memories of Love

Memories of Love

The Selected Poems of Bohdan Boychuk

*Edited by Mark Rudman
and translated by David Ignatow and Mark Rudman in
collaboration with the author*

THE SHEEP MEADOW PRESS
Riverdale-on-Hudson, New York

All inquiries and permission requests should be addressed to: The
Sheep Meadow Press, P.O. Box 1345, Riverdale-on-Hudson, New York
10471.

Library of Congress Cataloging-in-Publication Data

Boychuk, Bohdan.
  Memories of love.

  Translated from Ukrainian.
  1. Boychuk, Bohdan—Translations, English.
I. Rudman, Mark.   II. Ignatow, David, 1914–
III. Title.
PG3969.B57M46   1989   891.7'91   88-34840
ISBN 0-935296-76-X

Printed in the United States of America

Acknowledgments

Some of these poems have appeared in the following journals and anthologies:

A Celebration for Stanley Kunitz: "Late Spring," "You Came"

Confrontation: "Women," "The Evening"

Frank: "The Green Light in Aschaffenburg"

Grand Street: "Landscapes," "Stone Women," "Look into the Faces of Dead Poets"

Pequod: "Taxco," "You Came," "The Blind Bandura Players," "Five Poems On One Theme," "Snapshots from Airports," "Letters," "Almost a Lullaby"

Translation: "Three Dimensional Love" (4, 8, 10, 16)

2PLUS2: "Three Dimensional Love" (1,2,3,5,6,7,9,11,13,14,15)

The translators would like to thank Rachel Hadas, Donna Masini, and Stanley Moss for their careful criticism of the manuscript.

Contents

Introduction   7

I

Three Dimensional Love   16

II

The Blood of the Forests   50
Graves   51
Stone Women   52
The Blind Bandura Players   53
A Noon   54
Third Fall   55
The Evening   56

III

Embattled Garden   58
Letters   59
A Fairy Tale   61
Prescriptions for Solitude   64
Rue   67
A Single Woman   68
Married Couples   69
Almost a Lullaby   70
A Journey after Loves   71
A Nun   74
For My Mother   75
Old Age   77
Look into the Faces of Dead Poets   78
Five Poems on One Theme   80
You Came   83

IV

The Green Light in Aschaffenburg   86

Landscapes   87
Snapshots from Airports   88
A Snapshot with My Sons   90
One More Snapshot from the Airport   91
Late Spring   92
Taxco   93
A Short Journey   94
A Summer Mass   96
The Stone and Spring   97
A Lamp   98
A Lake   99
A Mirror   100

About the author   101
About the translator   101

Introduction

Bohdan Boychuk was born in 1927 in a small peasant village in the Western Ukraine. In an autobiographical sketch he describes his childhood as "rich in poverty, simplicity, and the beauty of nature." But this pastoral situation, that "delicate balance of survival" was tilted by the events of World War II. Captured by the Germans, he spent the last months of the war doing hard labor. The next four years he spent in a Displaced Persons camp in Aschaffenburg, West Germany, where he completed his high school education. In 1949 he came to America and enrolled in the City College of New York.

Bohdan Boychuk belongs to one of two main traditions of modern Ukrainian poetry. The first one, represented in the work of Pavlo Tychyna (1891–1967), is characterized by a soft lyricism, intricate musicality, and striking imagery. The second one is dramatic, with powerful intellectual metaphors, and heavy sharp-edged language, as in the poetry of Mykola Bazhan (1904–83), or bleak and tragic, as in the work of Todos Osmachka (1895–1962). Bohdan Boychuk comes closer to the second impulse, but nearer Osmachka's tragic peasant world in his early poems and more toward contemporary American and English poetry in his recent work.

Ukrainian literature began in the eleventh century with the famous epic poem *Prince Igor's Campaign*. Parallel to that an oral folk tradition existed, developing to the twentieth century. Both roots, written and oral, influenced and shaped Boychuk's poetry.

Ukrainian literature differs geo-culturally from other Slavic literatures: neither western nor eastern in character or style, it has some character of both. As in Boychuk's poetry, Ukrainian literature is deeply grounded in historical memory where past and present are equally available, equally significant. It provides symbols and myths that are as real as everyday occurrences.

Ukrainian poets, according to Boychuk, struggle against a double annihilation, in their person and in the death of their culture. To be a Ukrainian poet is "to be condemned, looking into death's eye." The poet is like a blind bandura player whose role is to open our eyes to our personal and social reality:

> They go through the steppes
> and with a cane of songs
> they feel their way
>
> they stamp
> the dry hardened soil
> of conscience
> look through the night
> with the big eyes of banduras*
> and show us
> the blinded ones
> the roads to ourselves

(The Blind Bandura Players, M.R.)

In Ukrainian literary circles, within a population of forty million speakers of Ukrainian, Bohdan Boychuk is one of the most widely appreciated living poets. His six books of poetry have rejuvenated modern Ukrainian poetry both here and in the Ukraine. He has also written two novels, eight plays and directed, as dynamic and controversial literary editor, the fine Ukrainian magazine *Suchasnist.* He has also co-edited (with Bohdan Rubchak) *Coordinates,* the most influential anthology of modern Ukranian poetry. In addition to his own writing he has translated such different poets as E.E. Cummings, Samuel Beckett, Juan Ramón Jiménez, and a number of contemporary American poets such as Stanley Kunitz, Robert Lowell, Stanley Moss, Katha Pollitt, and Mark Strand, as well as David Ignatow and myself. This close acquaintance with recent American poetry has opened his style.

Before we began to translate the poems in *Memories of Love* Bohdan and I had translated the Ukrainian poets Bohdan Antonych, Mykola Bazhan, and Ivan Drach, as well as Boris Paster-

---

*A bandura is a Ukrainian lute.

8

nak's *My Sister—Life*. We enjoyed the tug of war between cultures and languages. The three of us shared dissatisfactions that kept us alert. Because he is an expert translator as well as a poet, Bohdan knows that there are sacrifices, compensations, and impossibilities. These versions are true "face to face" collaborations. There were no "literals." Friendships deepened.

No sooner had he started classes at the University after coming to America than he was "invited" into the Korean War, and would have served but for the fact that tuberculosis was detected. Boychuk began writing poetry during his prolonged stay in a sanatorium.

Boychuk is not a cosmopolitan poet. No matter how closely observed his poems about Ukrainian peasant life, myth, and ritual may seem, they were written from a distance of time and space. These are not "snapshots," like several later poems that bear that title, rather we have a history of desire. Desire in Boychuk's work includes a concealed longing for his mother country. The early mythic poems are both metaphysical and deeply personal; humanly centered without being biographical.

They tumble across the ages
flattening the years into coffin planks
stained by prayers and hope
covered by candle wax and despair
buried in wreaths of pain
graves·
black wounds on the palms of earth
black holes under the rib of time
black eyes under your forehead

(*Graves*, D.I.)

In poems like *A Noon, Graves,* and *Stone Women*, what the Ukrainian critic Danylo Struk calls Boychuk's "metaphorization of reality" is most complete. These early poems contain few traces of the World War II ordeal he had undergone, nothing of direct devastation except the pain. Their mortal taint evokes the eternal. Their impersonality, as in oral literatures, represents a kind of ritualized mask. Boychuk makes no rhetorical flourish toward affirmation yet life itself is miraculous.

> Spring lightning strikes
> the face of a church, carving it
> into branching ivy.

> Green prayer
> overflows the walls,
> the stones.

(*The Stone and Spring*, D.I.)

Though Boychuk, in confronting the specific uncertainties of his existence, may embrace hopelessness as the only possible aesthetic act, he never gives up the search for meaning. He never becomes habituated to his fate as an exile. His torment retains its edge. Awareness is all that stands between him and emptiness. Urgency here breeds pithiness.

The Ukrainian poet Vasyl Barka rightly refers to Boychuk's "courageous, severe, lyrical style." Early poverty left its stylistic mark on him. There is an ascetic side to his allegiance to the lyric: Each word must carry its own weight. As in peasant life everything is used. Boychuk's poems relentlessly strip away the object from the stream of life. Even his dreams have the hard edge of form. Some of them read like folk poetry filtered through a modernist lens. Boychuk's poetry is the product of a distinctive voice which is as lyrical as it is bleak, as haunted as it is isolated:

> Landscapes pass through you
> on your right groves cast shadows over you
> on your left you are soaked
> with cold moonlight

fields draw you toward the horizon

the horizontal streets and canals
the vertical heights and lights
run through you

you are divided by everything you meet
you are borrowed by everything you love

(Landscapes, M.R.)

This poetics reduces man to a skeletal self, an abstract persona.
And his emphasis on only what is essential makes Boychuk one
of the least loquacious of poets. He refuses to linger on a word.
He favors poems that enact quick entrances, quick exits.

you came

without knowing why you'll leave

lost your feelings
without knowing why you loved

lost your body
without knowing why you lived

and you leave
without knowing why you came

(You Came, M.R.)

Boychuk is an existential poet with a religious edge: his vision
of life is spun out of the absence of religion, the absence of god.
He interrogates "the creator" about the meaning of his creation
yet trembles in front of the unknown: "Remembrance is closer to
us than life, which stands like a stranger on the road. I'm scared
by the unknown. The Creator did not give us a shred of His
heart." (*Letters,* M.R.)

His language, in most cases, is simple, direct, transparent. He desperately wants to hold chaos at bay. Imagination here is never an adjunct to experience; in this we see Boychuk's connection to other Slavic and Eastern European poets. He shares with Tadeusz Różewicz, the late Janos Pilinsky and Vasko Popa, a trust in imagination and a humility in the face of the unspeakable.

> Whoever   has   a   voice
> calls
> toward children
> but his voice sinks
> into their bodies
>
> calls toward parents
> but his voice shakes and
> tilts them under ground

(Five Poems on One Theme, D.I.)

I think that *Three Dimensional Love* is the central triumph of the book and one of the great modern poetic sequences. It mixes the songlike quatrain, free verse, and prose poem, and the sections break down loosely into erotic, existential and historic themes.

The first section, written in irregularly rhymed quatrains, deals with erotic ravings. The future tense reigns over these adolescent reveries. The second section confronts the monotony of daily life and sexual routines. Written in free verse, it portrays modern man, islanded in Manhattan, with no suitable outlet for his desire; lust turns to ashes in his mouth, a continuous "expense of spirit in a waste of shame." And the vivid, dramatic prose poetry of the third section documents his search for the meaning of life through love amid the Holocaust. Desiring redemption, he's left with love. He recounts the events that gave rise to the poem in his *Autobiographical Sketch.* "Shortly before the war, when I was still in the public school in Monastyryska, I fell in love with a Jewish girl. I do not remember her name, but to this very day I clearly see her image: she was a very delicate slim girl with a dark complexion, with big black eyes, and long black

12

hair smoothly combed and tied at the back. Her features were sharply but finely drawn. And she always dressed with great elegance. To me, an underclothed and undernourished peasant boy, she looked like a creature from a better world, unapproachable. For that reason I could never overcome my shyness and inferiority complex to reveal my feeling toward her. Actually, I could never utter a word to her. Later, during the German occupation, I constantly worried about that girl. On my way to school I would look for her among those lined up to be executed on Railroad Street, hoping not to find her. I looked for her everywhere else, hoping to find her. I still look for her."

Three Dimensional Love, far from being another poem about the Holocaust, locates its crisis in a timeless, universal problem: the futility of trying to heal the gap between subject and object, man and nature, which intertwine. But the subject, the poet's consciousness, is spewed out more ravaged after this entangled embrace than he began.

I always dreamt of her body. Now she was naked, entering the river. Delicate legs over white stones and a freckled girl. Slowly she waded into the river, assuming strange shapes under the currents. She went deeper and deeper, until she embraced the sun with both hands and, with a hazy smile, swam toward me.

In my home on Railroad Street, the empty walls, like blank pages, like God's merciless hands, weighed down on me each night. Human shadows twisted inside those walls, pushed out their emaciated faces and shouted into the dark.

(*Three Dimensional Love,* 3, section 3, M.R.)

He never knew her, never found her, never stopped searching for her, acting out the implicit contradictions of the human condition. His search for the girl could stand as a metaphor for all of his work. No answers are ever forthcoming, but Boychuk, refusing consolation, keeps the dialogue alive. And that, somehow, is enough.

Mark Rudman
April, 1988

I

Three Dimensional Love

One

1

When you stretch out in the shade
of a eucalyptus
the sun will begin to fade
above the hazy creek;

you'll wait through the sultry night
cooling your body in grass
dreaming of the girl in the light
sunburned and fresh.

2

drained of memory
you tumble
down into abandoned quarters
through rust-eaten
beams

the broken windows
stretch toward you
like pierced hands
through which
the soot sifts in

that's why in the day
you are compelled to think of
at night to look for

women

3

On summer afternoons I used to go to Raven Hill, which hung over the Strypa River outside of Buchach. In a sacristy of the ruined monastery, among the relics of saints, I waited for her. The hill towered above and the sun rolled down the slope into the river, flaring and skipping over the stones.

During the nights I was haunted by empty buildings with broken doors, with holes instead of windows, with the shadows of executed Jews. The walls in those buildings peeled, like scabby hands. They terrified my dreams. They flattened my innocent youth.

Two

1

Stretched on a fallen vine
that creeps between your ribs
nurturing pain
you will dream of her body;

that a pomegranate—one bite
will inflame your throat
and girls will emerge from out
of the thickets of a grove.

2

you anticipate
cracking hands
which push toward you
through the walls
cracking fingers
which crawl through the cracks
of your room
like spiders
pluck chunks
of your flesh
tear pieces of your sex

to keep death
at bay

3

Sensing her footsteps, the severe faces of the broken saints softened and their incantations sank into my bones. When she appeared, we tore off our clothes in the sacristy. I loved her girlish body, fresh as a path of white flowers. Her slim legs, narrow hips, unripe breasts. We hid our clothes behind a rock and ran toward the Strypa River.

At night Gestapo bullets pierced the dark; the cries of women and children leaked into my room through bullet holes: Trembling hands pushed through my walls, and begged for mercy.

Three

1

You will dream that birch-white leaves
will cup her whitening breasts,
wrap around her hips and caress
her legs;

you'll dream of burdock leaves,
their sap pressing against her thighs,
lifting her toward you
on flat green hands.

2

you dream of whitewashed walls
that like empty pages
would accept you
and your blue-eyed girl

but you're strangled
by long streets
propositioned by men
on 42nd St

plastered by
naked breasts
sweating hips
swollen lips

until the walls
flatten you at midnight
on the used woman's body
and a dirty mattress

like God's palms

3

I always dreamt of her body. Now she was naked, entering the river. Delicate legs over white stones and a freckled girl. Slowly she waded into the river, assuming strange shapes under the currents. She went deeper and deeper, until she embraced the sun with both hands and, with a hazy smile, swam toward me.

In my one room on Railroad Street, the empty walls, like blank pages, like God's merciless hands, weighed down on me each night. Human shadows twisted inside those walls, pushed out their emaciated faces and shouted into the dark.

Four

1

Spreading the night,
she'll lie beside you,
wet flowers will sprout in her mouth
and moisten your lips;

she'll lean on her side,
and nuzzle closer: the flowers
in her mouth will scald your mouth—
in the blinding darkness.

2

you rip off your damp shirt
enter concrete veins
and circulate
through the city's system

iron joints and ribs
rough stone and brick
stairs cages door-frames

ending in a sleazy room
with a bed and a basin of water
the smell of plastic flowers
and a naked woman in bed

3

Water foamed under the rocks. She was spreading her legs as the waves huddled around them. She was shimmering toward me with the sun, words trembling on her lips like a blue periwinkle.

Machine guns tore into the night, terror flashed, whitening the dark streets and squares. Heavy German boots stepped over the city's concrete veins. People crawled through the sewage canals. And in a gray room stood a dark bed, a basin with cold water, and the absent woman's form stretched over the bedspread.

Five

1

She'll lean over, inhale you
into the black fumes of her hair,
you will drink her whispering
like air;

you will gasp
on her youthful body,
as she lifts and plaits
you into her braid.

2

merciful sister
she leans
and presses
the pierced window panes
to your forehead

worn faces
drooping breasts
disjointed hips
seeping down
into your loneliness

you stand alone
in this apocalyptic city
inhaling the fumes
of bodies worn out
from making love

3

She was bending over the wind, spreading her golden hair. Water washed through her fingers, and as it washed off their warmth they became more tender, more transparent. Her lips flowered under the sun and I had an uneasy feeling: that she was murmuring her favorite plain song about parting.

It was mostly done. The sidewalks were already tombstones. The torsos of the executed hung from the shattered windows, their gaping mouths shouting voicelessly. On the narrow streets around St. Nicholas Church, I could hear moans and wheezes, the death rattles of the victims. Then night covered them with fog, poured liquid glass into their eyes.

Six

1

When petals freckle her face
like a flowerbed in June,
and mallow sprout from her hips
and squeeze you

then a flower storm blows you
down, under the night sky,
where, drenched, flood-dazzled,
you'll drown inside her eyes.

2

her body
is a trampled path
when the moon falls
on the planks of the scaffold
breaks and spills
like a yolk over the walls
each night
an ache gnaws
between her legs
like a lost hope

and so she saves herself
by making love to you

      and others

she brings salvation
by accepting you

      and others

3

A patch of light caressed her sex. As if to bury her, flowers crawled over her hair, her lips, her eyes.

The moon bruised its sides against the ruins of a castle and spilled over the roofs of St. Nicholas Hill. Between the vacant corridors a pale whore wandered, guardian of those who had to die, road for those who had to depart.

Seven

1

She'll spread her voice, embrace
you, numb your senses,
infect your innocence with lust
and weaken your defenses;

she'll come, wrap you in whispers,
spread her tender hands apart
for her frightened braids to creep
and coil inside your heart.

2

you enter
voiceless she sinks
into the sweat-stained bed

your eyes are blurred
by sooty houses
and asthmatic squares

plaster
sticks to your body
like sweat
and you give yourself

to her
in sacrifice
faithful and betrayed

she grips you
sinks with you
into her bed

you're troubled
by her snake-like braids

3

As she sang quietly, her voice spilled over her breasts. When I bent over her startled braids, she cooled my face with whispers.

The dead wailed on the Town Hall Tower as men in uniforms, sunk in asphalt, carrying death, carved out the hour with machine guns. The dying lay scattered over the hillside, shouts poled out of their throats. The moon staring into the whites of their eyes.

Eight

1

When her image shakes your senses
and aching for her caresses
rips into your flesh;
when she lashes

you with passion,
with the flax of her voice,
when she rinses you in laughter,
you'll have no choice.

2

when your senses are pummeled
by deaf neighborhoods
blind entrances
hobbled corridors
loved and loveless
wives

when memories
no longer pass
through the flattened mind
then you are forced to live now

condemned and condemning
some woman
for one night
of love

3

When the sun fell behind her plaited hair she trembled and as she clutched me I felt her dissolving and circulating in my veins.

Leaden ghettos pressed down the memory of the executed. Only the dead eyes, filled with white moonlight, rolled down the hill from the Jewish cemetery into the Strypa River. The enraged castle yanked skeletons from its walls and hurled them over the numb city, like curses.

Nine

1

When night sneaks a glance
through the moon's monocle
into the endless dark
you will crave her

to lure you in her arms,
submerge you in her eyes
so that you a crying boy
will be lost in her sweet center.

2

when the night falls
formless into the streets
you want to drown
in her caress

to hold on
to her body
that thin plank of hope
like a boy
drowning
in death

3

Her face shone under me and her stiff nipples pressed into my flesh. Her belly, like a frightened bird, fluttered against my hips, her legs squeezed my waist. The evening spilled the white of its solitary eye over our bodies.

The night, torn apart by bullets, hung over the precipice. The Gestapo stunned the black holes in the walls with swastikas instead of faces, heavy boots thumping over the cobblestones, hunting for those still alive. When they pulled them out, the moon caught in the victim's throats and they could not shout into the vanquished world.

Ten

1

Her long back
will whiten through the night
like a crack
in a dark wall,

the cleft
of her absence
through which
you will fall.

2

her body
whitens
through the night

you
push yourself through
cataracting alleys

till finally you fall
exhausted
into her
faithlessness

3

The coolness of the evening condensed on our skin and we had to run up Raven Hill toward the monastery. To our right a young creek beat its sides against roots and fell headlong, like a reckless boy, into the Strypa River. I had an urge to lift her up in my arms, carry her into the sacristy and beg the faded saints to protect her.

When I returned from school, the Gestapo led the condemned to the Jewish cemetery, handed out shovels and forced them to dig a hole. Around noon, when the ditch was ready, they lined them up along the edge and shot. Dry dirt fell over them, filling their frightened eyes. The dead women's hair moaned under the clotted earth and rose on the wind like a passing epitaph.

Eleven

1

She'll shed the night's percale,
burn your lips with her breasts,
infect your moistened eyes
with unrest,

you'll dip your anxious brow
in the white foam of her flesh,
turning to return
into her.

2

tearing apart her cotton dress
she crosses Times Square
and gives herself to everyone
who hungers for flesh
and pays

you
also make love to her
having no one
closer

3

In the monastery dusk covered her nipples. Dressed, we stood next to each other and listened to the Strypa below, to the stars over the precipice. We were alone and happy. But the saints, who kept holding on to their faded eternity on the ruins, pushed out their fierce faces through the walls and did not rejoice with us.

After the night Action on the Jews, as the Gestapo chased over the empty streets, hunting and shooting, I was headed down Railroad Street to the Commercial School. Near Sobiesky Well I saw a woman fallen in the middle of the street with her arms spread. Her head had been splintered by a bullet. Her hair was dark brown. At her side lay an opened handbag, spilling pins, beads, combs . . .

Twelve

1

You'll dip your brow in white . . .
go down between her legs,
contracting and contracted,
by the mysteries of flesh,

dizzied by reveries
you'll feel her heavy breath
convulse and plunge you down
into her element.

2

you fade
on afternoon's paper
leaf through the pages
assigned to you
unwritten
blank

discouraged
you sink
between cold naked knees

3

The next afternoon I was waiting for her in the sacristy. The sun rolled down the steep hill and fell into the river which contracted in the heat and skipped over the rocks. But she did not appear. The sun cooled off in the river, went down in white convulsions. A chunk of moonlight glittered on the water, but she did not appear.

St. Nicholas Church was ringed by buildings with empty rooms, stolen doors. In the Jewish Cemetery terrified braids crawled to the wind. A girl's white hand protruded from the ground, as if waving goodbye to me. . . .

Thirteen

1

She will fill you, rock you,
deepening your need,
but you won't find yourself—
just an ache.

2

every morning and night the same
rush toward whitewashed
offices and homes

an emptiness in which
only lust remains
carrying you toward
her mysterious
cruel sex

3

On the third day I kept waiting for her on Raven Hill, but she did not come. When the dark descended I got scared and ran back to the city. The house where she lived stood open. I ran from room to room, calling her, but only the echo of my voice came back. Seized by a nauseating feeling of terror, I felt as if I were hurtling into her absence.

Day after day I haunted offices, searching for her. I filled out questionnaires which called for me to describe her, but I could not do it because every time I had met her she was more beautiful and, therefore, stranger to me. Exhaustion tired my legs. Discouraged, I would go outside the town to the executed. But I couldn't find her there.

Fourteen

1

Your voice will thicken in your mouth,
convulsions lock your bones—
finally you enter her as day
breaks down.

2

having rubbed your face
against city walls
having pulled your sense
of touch off your skin
you dull your sight
against time
and your tongue
grows numb

you spread yourself
on her bare belly
she throws her arms
around your neck
and chokes you

3

I looked for her in the Jewish cemetery, looked in the memories of our friends, looked for a trace of her touch on the walls, for her kisses on my body. But the memories faded, the touches peeled off, her lips had been erased from my skin. And I was left with myself.

I felt nothing now. And left my town so that I would not see people with numbed tongues, would not see shadows pressed into the walls, would not hear the silence that choked our homes.

Fifteen

1

She will scoop out
your tenderness with lust,
and make you grieve for her
and wait forever.

2

you embezzle your feelings
beds like graves
like sins
without absolution
repel you

walls lean over
to bury you alive

3

Did her beauty startle the moon? Did flowers grow from her palms? Did the wind inhale her hair . . . ? Or did she hide, to make me long for her till Judgment Day?

I stepped over men in uniforms who had lost their motion, and stared into the sky; I wiped off the dirt with my hand and looked into the blue faces of the dead; I squeezed through the barracks with striped people and looked into the holes of crematoria pouring out fumes into the world of unabsolved sins. And I felt that she was close.

Sixteen

1

You will gasp
upon the dawn's dead fires,
at last feeling no need for her:
no passion or desire.

2

the heat
exhausts the streets
the time
strikes
the top of the city's
shaved head

you choke
on silence
lime fills
your mouth
bowels
veins

you feel no pain
no emptiness
no loneliness
no joy

3

A final silence collected in the glassy eyes of the dead. I was the only one who kept on walking over the earth of her absence, with the presence of the shadows of the executed, with the holes of crematoria. Why did I have to endure it? In the final account, the monastery on Raven Hill was a betrayal. The woman near Sobiesky Well—a betrayal. The bodies over the planks of Buchenwald—betrayal. My witnessing was also a betrayal. I'm alive.

M.R.

II

The Blood of the Forests

Here the wind soaked the oak-bark,
lashed it with the hair of bronze girls
who warmed the midnight songs around bonfires
trampling a dance into the ground.
        The bronze bodies
           softened, the girls,
        weaving their fate
          into garlands,
      melted under
        the men's bodies,
       in the young bushes.
Then the women
gathered bundles of shadows
and, leaving their footprints behind,
began the long journey through the cells of
violets, cherry trees, and oaks.

M.R.

50

Graves

They tumble across the ages
flattening the years into coffin planks
stained by prayers and hope
covered by candle wax and despair
buried in wreaths of pain
graves
black wounds on the palms of earth
black holes under the rib of time
black eyes under your forehead

D.I.

Stone Women*

Sunk to their thighs in graves
they push the shadows of the dead
back into earth

From the white wonder of bones
their sex turned to stone
will not tremble at night
from a touch of your hand

D.I.

*Stone statues on burial mounds, scattered by nomadic tribes over the steppes
between the sixth and thirteenth centuries.

The Blind Bandura Players*

They go through the steppes
and with a cane of songs
they feel their way

they stamp
the dry hardened soil
of conscience
look through the night
with the big eyes of banduras*
and show us
the blinded ones
the roads to ourselves

M.R.

*Bandura is a musical instrument with 30 or more strings. It was played in the
sixteenth and seventeenth centuries by the blind Bandurists who were also news
carriers.

A Noon

Under the hot sun
the fields swell;
women
sticky with sweat
bend over their sickles
tilting the sunburned jugs
of their breasts
and sink into stubble.

D.I.

Third Fall

Sun withers
on a bland sky,
woods yellowing,

smell acrid,
permeating the huts,
choking the sheaves.

From over the horizon the wind
inclines the tall women,
left behind in the fields.
They push their pregnant bellies
into the coming years.

D.I.

The Evening

Fever scorches the earth
which lies breathing heavily
with dusk pulled over its eyes.

Under the burlap sky
the full moon rounds,
and the earth grows light.

Men drift toward women
whose hips grow into clay huts.
And their hearts grow light.

M.R.

III

Embattled Garden

to Martha Graham

They both are lonely in the garden.
Over the meadow beyond the green path
the yellow moon tilts
and spills the white light onto earth,

there naked men and women
rip off their shadows
and lie down for the full moon
to melt their thighs and arms.

Adam and Eve both cross to this side
of the path.
Their throats grow a rough hempen voice
where snakes in the trees await them.

D.I.

Letters

We are strangers, because nobody defiled you with a name. We met on the night's black waters, you came over the soft path of a dream. Waters trembled and receded like a tide. And I don't know you, because nobody defiled you with a name. You are pure. For a name is a stain, blurred with many meanings. I'm glad I do not know you.

Hartford, Jan. 1
The hours elbow me, but I don't want to go. It's frightening. The hours push and shove me out the old year, but I refuse to go, hold on to my memories and think of you. It's frightening to step into the unknown. Remembrance is closer to us than life, which stands like a stranger on the road. I'm scared by the unknown. The Creator did not give us a shred of His heart.

Washington, March 11
The season reminds me of you: green buds rise through the black shirt and disturb me with the smells of spring. Vegetation swells with sap, yearns to grow—for just one spring, one summer! Oh, what a narrow time! But my spring is only a memory. My spring is you. Maybe it is better that you remain a memory, because we don't know how to forgive when a woman's beauty wears down with age.

Sarasota, Aug. 1

Heat. Excess of sun wrongs and scorches. Biting fruits, we infect our mouths with a taste of death; smells of late love. I never bit your mouth. The songs of your hips are also unknown to me. After having drunk a loved woman, do we really lose our deepest feelings for her? I don't know. I never wronged your lips, we never knew the smell of late love.

New York, Sept. 11

I was looking for you on the streets of New York. A hopeless search. The streets choked with faces, swollen with weariness, boredom, stale loves. Time smeared the faces with sweat and wrinkles, drove them closer to the end of the last street. You were not there. Time cannot mark a dream by age. You will never change. You will be young.

. . . .

Heaven is dumb to creatures. The shouts of planets, marked by God, say nothing. We stretch our roads over gelatinous space and they strangle us. We lose our footprints and grieve for a touch (does it matter?) of your white hand, for the beauty (does it?) of a dark-eyed (does it?) glance, for the penetration of a girl's body. Then we have to learn how to forget. Everything.

M.R.

A Fairy Tale

Once upon
she was the only child,
called Princess.

> *you came to me*
> *in spring,*
> *your bare feet*
> *warmed*
> *violet buds*
> *to bloom.*

When Princess' father and mother
went on a journey,
never to return,
she befriended her walls
and talked to them.
The walls listened
for they loved her soft voice.

> *wind in the clearing*
> *tried to suck*
> *your youthful*
> *breasts,*
> *to blow away*
> *your beauty.*

The neighbors envied
the Princess' solitude:
they sent a witch to take
her walls away, to breathe
a bad spell on her eyes, lips, ears,
and Princess became blind,
lost her voice, became deaf.

inflamed mouths,
spattered with red,
hurled curses
on our love.

Young Princess lay at the crossroad
in the shadow of a tree.
The years passed by, trampling her
into the ground.

I embraced you
and we took
what ripened for us
under the moon,
so kiss me
once more.

Then came the Prince.
With his glance he nailed
the witch to a pole,
recovered Princess' home
and came to the crossroads.
With a breath he opened
Princess' eyes and ears,
returned her speech.
Her white arms
like two roads
stretched toward him.

kiss me, for soon
the wind will blow
your beauty away
and cold will flow out
of your heart.

They lived on opposite sides
of the road
to the end of their time.

Sometimes happy.

D.I.

Prescriptions for Solitude
for Maria

1

When you are gone
your absence
sucks me in,
grows,
and I lose direction,
identity.

2

When I think of you
warmth and brightness
penetrate the wrinkles
of my soul,
cracks
of my thoughts,
cells
of my body.

Then I refuse to think
about the future.

Then
I forget
to grieve.

3

Swallowing
the last drops of sleep
I stretch out my arm
and feel the form
of your absent body
in my bed.

I bend over
and kiss its lips,
but it doesn't move.

How much love
do I need
to bring it
to life?

4

Restless,
I take off
my loneliness
and go out.

Women
cover me up with
sympathetic glances,
girls
avert their faces.

Looking
into a window pane
I realize
I am naked.
For my loneliness
was all the clothing
I wore
without you.

5

I try
to imagine you,
but landscapes
you entered
are hard to
imagine.

People
with whom you stay
are too distant.

So I keep rearranging
your image
one landscape
to another,
one setting
to another—
each time
a bit closer
to me.

6

All signs
I notice lately
are good:
time changes its course
and moves
toward you,
distance
over the eastern horizon
whitens and
becomes translucent,

memory
brightens
and recreates your
finest features,

even I
shake off my years
and move
toward you.

M.R.

Rue

For R.

November stars
don't care
about love.

Falling, they separate themselves
from the sky,
and us from each other.

Groping through the stars
I lose sense
of woman's body,
forget the smell of rue
that intoxicated the spring,
and enter the trembling
of a yellowed leaf.

D.I.

A Single Woman

In a trunk she stored
the dowry of her youth
and kept luring men, until
her braid was soaked in gray.

D.I.

Married Couples

The years snuff out
our senses,
exhaust our affections.

Events bury memory
and couples sink
into speechless indifference.

You know your beauty
will not last,
will you have enough love
to stay afloat
on words?

M.R.

Almost a Lullaby

Mommy, will the sun sleep on that pine?
Yes, my son, upon its branches.
And keep the maybugs warm?
Yes, and the beetles.
Will father come back tonight from the war?
Yes. . . . From under the distant earth.
As soon as the sun sets?
As soon as the dark sets in.
You said it's easier for him to walk in the dark.
Yes, my dear, the daylight hurts his eye sockets.
He'll really come tonight?
Go to bed. He'll come to you.
Keep the light on for him to find his way.
I'll light a candle for him.
Will father bring some golden bugs
that crawl the sky at night?
Go to bed. He'll catch a few for you.
He should be careful not to break the moon.
He knows his way in heaven.
Will father also pick some flowers for you?
Sleep, my son, sleep . . .

M.R.

A Journey after Loves

1

ripe years redden ahead
clustered questions
grow gray

over a footbridge
I cross toward autumn
and gather loves'
remains

2

flowers wither
into dusk
with their seasonal aches
my mouth sore from bitter fruit
October weather
cools at my heart

3

my memories are like the spasms
of roads to nowhere
my memories are like faded trails
scars

4

all roads led to you
but you led nowhere
taking me along
refusing yourself

all roads were you
but you were none

5

I choked on your body
happiness soared through me
leaving an incurable need
to seek my cure in women
who drink me out in lust

6

I gave myself away
becoming absent in myself
I gave myself to women
sending sons toward the future

now a single illusion remains
of life in my children
like a stale liquid
in my mouth

7

my life is torn into strophes
of love and betrayal
my life is covered by signs
of deep delusions

with every penetration
of woman's body
I contracted within myself
becoming distant

8

now I stand in the wind
scoured through
at the graying edge of age

I gave myself away
along the road

D.I.

A Nun

Into the black silk
she carefully wraps
her breasts
and the ripeness of her womb

with her white fingertips
she moves her days
like rosary beads
and places her feelings
like flowers
between the yellowed leaves
of the breviary

and all her life
washes her hands
in whispered prayers
to stretch them out
unblemished
toward a chalice
and salvation

forgetting
to give alms
to a beggar

unknown woman rest
let your eternity be kind
and caring

M.R.

For My Mother

1

For everything:
a withered lilac bush,
a clod of clay.

Nothing more.

For a ripped yell
on a bed of birth,
for pain
knotting your insides,
for moans,
and for the baby
between your knees
bursting with a loud cry.
For everything.

2

With hands
like dead branches
you swept through
your days,
alone,
and at your feet
your life,
a hungry dog,
bristled and growled.

3

Tears streaming from
under your eyebrows
burned me.

How can I sing out of me
my mother's tears,
how can I moan a song
of skeletal bones,
yellow hands,
red cough,
and something, like love,
warm in her chest.

4

I've seen an icon over her head,
a myrtle in the window,
a black box.

5

And I brought her
a withered lilac bush,
a clod of clay.

Nothing more.

For I have sorrow,
only a red cough,

and something warm in my chest
like love.

D.I.

Old Age

So few memories,
too few to forget. . .
so hard to see
in an empty room
so hard to cross
into another empty room;

autumns
russled through
my fingertips,
springs
slipped through
my hands
and the warm-lipped
nights
with women. . .

so few
memories,
too few to
forget. . .
so hard to see
in an empty room
so hard to cross
into another
room.

D.I.

Look into the Faces of Dead Poets

The cheek bones protrude
the eye sockets empty and sunken
look into their gaping mouths
the words have turned to lime
look into their skulls
where the waters are dead thick

look into their faces
for you have to search behind the eyes
covered with cataracts
you have to reach beyond the ears
plugged with silence
you have to touch hair parting
from the skull
    arms and legs stiffened
    lump veins and nerves
    self-devouring cells
you have to penetrate the dead faces
you have to get to the absence of blood
you have to pause on the other shore of bones

to see

how they press themselves into your memory
with their Gods

with the horror at separating
from the nakedness of women
how their words drill
for openings through their deaths

but you

stare into their faces
stroke your plump women

feed

D.I.

Five Poems on One Theme

1

W h o e v e r   c a n   s m e l l
inhales her braids
and is overcome by love

inhales her breath
and is softened
by her springtime

inhales her sex
and the hot clot of cells
terrifies him

2

W h o e v e r   c a n   t a s t e
tries the lips of a girl
and her tongue
fills his mouth
like a fruit

tries her eyes
and his mouth is filled
with warm tears

tries her body
and the salt of her life
seeps into his glands

3

Whoever has eyes
looks behind himself
looks in front of himself
looks inside himself
tries to penetrate
all times
and beyond time

and sees
as from behind the corner
his life
not lived
but passed by
like another's

4

Whoever has a voice
calls
toward children
but his voice sinks
into their bodies

calls toward parents
but his voice shakes and
tilts them under ground

5

Whoever has ears
presses them to the door
and hears the mother
as she splashes him out
of her womb

hears whispering girls
who caress him into
manhood

hears
incantations
which lead him out
of old age

to hear God
puts his ear to the coffin
and becomes deaf

D.I.

You Came

without knowing why you'll leave

lost your feelings
without knowing why you loved

lost your body
without knowing why you lived

and you leave
without knowing why you came

M.R.

IV

The Green Light in Aschaffenburg

Rooftiles shrink under green moss,
old houses float over
the surface of time;
another dawn wipes the shadows
rising like yeast
off the cobblestones.

An empty street whitens,
and a crowd
of featureless men
wait for the green light
to pass.

So they will wait
(though the street is clear)
till the corporal commands
new crematoria,
bones to moan:
They will wait till Judgment Day.

M.R.

Landscapes

Landscapes pass through you
on your right groves cast shadows over you
on your left you are soaked
with cold moonlight

fields draw you toward the horizon

the horizontal streets and canals
the vertical heights and lights
run through you

you are divided by everything you meet
you are borrowed by everything you love

M.R.

Snapshots from Airports

1. A Little Girl

I don't remember what she really looked like. Soft hair, a short dress (for the heat poured from all sides over the landscape and the people), playful eyes, freckled chirping—all of this will be to the point. For the girl was lively. For the girl was like any girl. All will be to the point. At the airport in Orlando or Los Angeles, I don't remember.

song for a girl: little flirt go on
                      wrap around your waist
                      summers springs and falls
                      and mornings of goodbyes

For the girl was seeing her father off. For the girl was proud. She danced around him, embraced him—she wanted everyone to see her tall handsome father in uniform. Circling she wished to wrap around her waist the whole world.

song for a soldier: o soldier march away
                      spreading for the worms
                      your greatcoat and your bones
                      in the morning mist

2. A Boy

He had a few minutes left before the flight. The boy held a girl by the hand and she kept on talking to him, smiling. The boy was sorry to part with her. She was not beautiful, she only smiled pleasantly. But the boy was sorry to part with her. Maybe he liked her naked body, making love to her. Maybe they never made love. Maybe he loved her smile, loved her. I don't know. It was too hard for me to cross those few steps into their souls.

song for lovers: when your youth
comes down like dew
make love before
life swallows you

3. A Woman

Those few minutes before the flight dragged on. The wife was seeing her husband off. Husband and wife, wife and husband—they stood in silence. For all words had been said and answered. All words had been used and misused. When the minutes came to the end, they plastered light kisses on each other's lips and separated: it was unpleasant to both of them.

song for married couples: no need to be bored
time goes by too fast
go and wash your words
go and rinse your hearts

4. An Old Man

Time rushed and the old man rushed, but couldn't keep up. He held onto a shaky arm of his old woman, but couldn't keep up. Those few minutes before the flight passed quickly. Though there was no need to hold hands, no need to kiss, the old man couldn't keep up.

song for the old: though wrinkles crawl and flow
down your trembling hands
hold on like once upon
or—for—ever—end

M.R.

A Snapshot with My Sons

I stand in an uncertain pose
between two tall sons,
as if pushed into the ground,
as if pushed back
toward the past.

The years,
like strangers
I might have passed
but did not greet,
crowd in my door.

And I stand in an uncertain pose,
not knowing
how to restrain the moan of blood,
how to get rid
of a young heart.

M.R.

One More Snapshot from the Airport

With each spring
women's hips are lovelier
but their smiles to me
are covered with a film
of indifference.

Their waists,
slimmer this year,
move like a song.

Excited
I start running back
and, like a boy,
jump over the years.

D.I.

Late Spring

In 1980
spring was late
in Georgia.

Only one bare tree
that I passed
had some buds
pushing through the bark,
like white blisters
bursting on the wind.

On my way back,
I failed to notice
that tree.

And I realized
that I was late into my life,
walking out of the landscape
and entering myself.

D.I.

Taxco

Time pauses halfway up—
gasps and collapses on the hill.
A dark-skinned Christ rides a donkey
with a poor man's face.

Hollow drums beat over
the clay skulls of the houses
whose spines grow into the rocks;
rooftiles melt and flow

down narrow streets. Time
finds it hard to come or go,
and the hands grasping for silver
stiffen in the deep earth.

M.R.

A Short Journey

1. Virginia

On azure sands
the watermelon's split;
the red blood pours
over plantations,

floods the huts
hurt by the rain,
waters the tobacco plants
and the pain in the roots
of acacias.

2. South Carolina

A black woman
hung over the well
her breasts,
with wounds
like cactuses;
dipping the pail,
scooping up the day,
she cried:
This day's so lonely, Lord,
and hard!
So hard!

3. *Georgia*

Dawn wet,
fog white.
Muffled voices
beat against the twigs:
dry is your land,
Lord,
dry, how dry!
It will dry our bodies,
it will dry our mouths:
and our bones will be white,
Lord,
they will be white
and the earth dry.

M.R.

A Summer Mass

Late summer
perished
on the fence,

sunflower candle
burned
and dripped
in the garden.

God sprinkled
from His holy hand,
but could not revive them.

D.I.

The Stone and Spring

Spring lightning strikes
the face of a church, carving it
into branching ivy.

Green prayer
overflows the walls,
the stones.

D.I.

A Lamp

brightens
but does not illuminate you
shines
but does not penetrate you
gives light
but does not quench the darkness

D.I.

A Lake

The lake
the mountain's
bottomless eye
looks upward
observing   sun   moon   stars
sometimes a bird's body
falls into its pupil
sometimes a woman's body
bathes in its retina

it takes them all in
without emotion

the mountain's indifferent eye

M.R.

A Mirror

Every day you disfigure
your mirror
force it
to reflect you
other than you are

and so you
double-up
turn yourself inside out
until the glass
disgusted
vomits you up
unloved
undone
unwanted

M.R.

Bohdan Boychuk is the author of six books of poetry in Ukrainian. He has also written two novels, eight plays and acted as editor of the Ukrainian literary magazine *Suchasnist*. He is the co-editor (with Bohdan Rubchak) of the major anthology of modern Ukrainian poetry, *Coordinates*. His poems have appeared in English in such journals as *Frank, Grand Street, 2PLUS2, Pequod*, and *Translation*. In addition to his own writing he has translated Samuel Beckett, E.E. Cummings, Juan Ramón Jiménez, and many contemporary American poets. He works as an engineer and lives in New York City.

David Ignatow has published thirteen volumes of poetry, two prose collections, and his *Notebooks*. He has received two Guggenheim fellowships, the Wallace Stevens Fellowship from Yale University and the Rockefeller Foundation Fellowship. His awards include the Shelley Memorial, and others from the National Institute of Arts and Letters, the National Endowment for the Arts, and the Bollingen Prize. He is visiting professor at Columbia University.

Mark Rudman's *By Contraries: Poems 1970–84* appeared in 1987. He has also published a book of criticism, *Robert Lowell: An Introduction to the Poetry*. He has received fellowships from the Ingram Merrill Foundation and the New York Foundation of the Arts, a P.E.N. Translation Fellowship and the Max Hayward Award from the Translation Center at Columbia University. He is adjunct professor at New York University and Columbia University.